THIN TIMES AND THIN PLACES

LIFE LESSONS FROM THE LABYRINTH

JOEL W. KREGER

ISBN 978-0-9889514-9-5
© 2013 Joel Kreger

DEDICATION

To all those who love and inspire me:
Kathy - my wife, friend, and lover in life
Rachel, Zachary, Joshua, Casandra - my children
Brooke, Joe, Christine - my children's partners
Kellan, Jaylee, Everly, Adalyn, Jaxon, Tenley, Lucy, and Naya - my grandchildren
Dear ones from work and play - my friends

FORWARD

A note about the labyrinths I walk: A decade and a half ago we were fortunate enough to be able to buy seventeen acres in beautiful northwestern Wisconsin, near a town called Cumberland. On this former hayfield we built our home and I considered what to do with the rest of the land. I ended up planting trees on some of it and mowing walking paths and labyrinths into the rest of it. I didn't anticipate that the labyrinths would have the effect on me that they did, at the time it just seemed like an interesting thing to do. But as often is the case in life, actions have unintended consequences. The labyrinths have taken me on a spiritual journey in the years that I have walked them. I write this book to share elements of that journey with you, and hope that in the sharing you might find pleasure and wisdom. This is a book about labyrinths, life, and love - though not necessarily in that order.

Labyrinths are human constructs that go far back in our history. They may vary in style from location to location, but they all reflect a dimension of our human spirituality. This book is not a book about the history, forms, or historic uses of labyrinths. It is a book about spirituality and how the labyrinths have deepened mine in some wonderful ways. It is intended to help us understand who we are.

Life is full of struggles, difficulties, successes, and celebrations. This book does not attempt to chronicle the full expanse of the human pathos and exaltation. It is intended to help us make some meaning of this journey by simple reflections that explore our living.

Love. God is love, and humanity is about love. This is not a book that is the final exposition describing love. It is intended to relate one simple soul's journey into the spiritual reality of love in the hope that it will help enlighten others.

This book is intended to be a resource for my fellow travelers. Not everyone has the opportunity to walk labyrinths on a regular basis, though I would certainly be one to advocate the practice, so what I have attempted to do is to share some of the lessons I have learned in my labyrinth walks in the hope that a reflection on them would give guidance and encouragement in others' spiritual walks.

So, please, take your time as you walk through these chapters. Let each one settle in over the course of a day and walk the labyrinth with me for a month.

These selections are taken from reflections I write after some of my walks. They are from a variety of times throughout the hours of the day, and the days of the year. I invite you to walk with me as you read these reflections.

1 - In the Field of Labyrinths

In the Field of Labyrinths

I am not sure where to begin. I certainly can't begin at the beginning - for I know not where that was. Nor can I start at the conclusion - for I know not where it will end. Sometime, during the course of my life, I encountered these mystical things called labyrinths. They are not mazes, or puzzles, for they have paths in and they have paths out. They are not meant to confuse, but to clarify. Some people meditate in stillness and silence. For me the movement through the labyrinth moves me through my thoughts.

I experience these labyrinths as "thin places". They are where the fabric between the material world and the spiritual world is "thin". As I walk into the labyrinth I take my humanity with me, and I am allowed to touch the depths of my soul. They let me delve to the core of who I am, what I am doing, why I am doing it. They help me see and understand myself more clearly as I walk deeper into the labyrinth. There I experience my humanity. But something else begins to happen. As I walk deeper into the labyrinth, I also experience the divine. I feel as though I touch the very face of God as I walk this path set in the beauty of this creation. The depths of my humanity touching the face of God. Thin place, indeed.

These labyrinths become places where I commune with God, the creation, and my fellow travelers in this existence, for when I walk the labyrinth my thoughts are also pulled into a reflection of the relationships I share with others. I begin to think longer and deeper about those with whom I share my life journey and my daily experiences. My steps become a prayer to enable me to touch them in meaningful and positive ways.

There is a Latin phrase "Solvitur ambulando" which, when translated is, "It is solved through walking." I find that many of the problems of my day, the troubles in my relationships, and the temptations in my soul, work their way out when I walk my journey through the labyrinth.

There is more to be said, but the time to say it is not now.

2 - THIN TIME

Sunrise on Vermillion Lake - just a few steps from one of the labyrinths I walk.

Previously I shared the thought about how, for me, labyrinths are "thin places". Tonight, allow me to make a brief comment on "thin times." Thin times are those moments when the veil between the spiritual and physical realms diminishes to such a degree as to become virtually non-existent. Perhaps you have noticed that sunrises and sunsets affect me in powerful ways. These are "thin times."

Tonight I experienced another moment of thin time. I went for a long walk late tonight in the light of the full moon. It wound up (figuratively and literally) being more than two hours - and I didn't want it to end.

As I walked in the crispness of this late November night and was bathed in the luminescence of the moonlight reflecting off the dusting of snow that lay softly in my field of labyrinths, the gossamer veil vanished in my mind and the universe was as one. I was blessed.

One of the first things that happened as I walked was that several deer circled around me. It made me reflect on "The Deer's Cry" also call the "Lorica" of St. Patrick (perhaps I have more Celtic blood in me than the wee bit of the Scot that I know about) and as I meditated on it, I was deeply humbled. I invite you to find and listen to Lisa Kelly of Celtic Woman sing a version of it.

Time was thinning.

Then as I walked the Trinity Labyrinth I noticed how still the night was. Not even a hint of wind stirred the air. Breathless. In that silence, I heard the wild geese calling as they gathered on the lake resting for the night from their migration and I was struck by our human need to move, to rest, and to gather together.

Time was thinning.

Then I noticed the moon in all it's fullness and glory. There was a haze of clouds in the sky which obscured the stars, but the moon pierced through them and created a stunning circle which ringed it taking up nearly a quarter of the heavens. I was so awestruck all I could do was to stand there for several moments, and say "Wow!" That was about as eloquent as I could be at the moment. As I said - awestruck.

Time was so thin it dissolved. That gossamer veil had disappeared. For a moment all was one.

3 - HORIZONS

Moonrise at Sunset

There was a delightful sunrise today. I could have sat still and just soaked it in minute after minute. But instead I walked the labyrinth.

As I twisted and turned throughout it, I was blessed to keep seeing that stunning sunrise come back into view. What a refreshing sight. Ahhh . . . but then I noticed something which had been there all time, but which somehow I had never seemed to realize before. When the labyrinth turned me around and I saw the far horizon, I gazed upon another scene of beauty. The beauty of the rising sun was reflected in softer, muted, gentler tones. Perhaps not as striking in that moment, but just as sensually delightful to my soul.

And I wonder, is this how we sometimes go through life? Do we focus on the one horizon? Do we let something catch and hold our eye, or our very being? Do we fail to see the beauty that lies in the other directions? Do we become so focused on certain goals, pleasures, and delights, that we miss experiencing the wonder that completely surrounds us?

The next time I pause to watch the sunrise, or the sunset, I will take the time to look in other directions and see the wonders which are revealed.

The next day that I walk through, I will no doubt have a focus for what I do, but I will also take the time to look around, revel in the wonder of it all, and allow it to fill my life.

Some days later . . .

So when I was walking tonight, what happened?
I experienced that magnificent moonrise on the one horizon as the sun was setting on the other. While the sun was setting golden in the western horizon, the moon was rising in an eastern horizon that was imbued with a soft dusky rose hue reflected from the distant setting sun. This was a time when one really must look in both directions to be immersed in the beauty of the moment.

Take the time, look around, let beauty and peace surround you and fill you.

4 - FOG

A Tree that Speaks to Me

There was a deepening fog which had descended upon the labyrinths as I walked late tonight, but yet there was enough light reflected through the mist to follow the paths. There was something about walking in the fog that triggered memories of a sermon I had written a couple of decades ago. It was written in verse and had as its foundation the poem "The Road Goes Ever On And On" by Tolkien in The Lord of the Rings, and the post resurrection story of the Road to Emmaus.

As I walked on and on through the fog, memories came to me of long ago times in my life - things I have not thought about in years. I started remembering moments during my life journey, and of how things often were unclear. Both those foundational writings mentioned earlier have times of travel and moments of uncertainty, and also moments of awareness and revelation in them. So does life. And then the journey goes on.

So as I came to the center of a labyrinth - I was hoping for something to happened. Something did. In the center of this labyrinth stands a pine tree that I planted as a seedling several years ago but which now stands ten feet tall. As I entered the center core of the labyrinth and approached the tree, the sounds around me changed. I could hear the still small voice of the pine as the barely perceptible breeze softly strummed the needles. I was close enough, almost standing in the arms of the tree, to hear its soothing song.

Then I stepped back, and the song was gone. For that moment when I was close, I heard the beauty of that song of nature. And then moving away to go on my journey it was gone. But the memory of it fills me still. And back I go on my road, ever on and on, and whither then, I cannot say.

But this I know, the epiphanies happen when we are open to them, and the memories of those moments carry us through our fog enshrouded lives.

5 - LOVE, AND DO WHAT THOU WILT

Sunrise with the Colors of Love

Normally I am hoping to empty myself when I walk, so that I may more fully experience the divine presence, but sometimes when I walk, the world and its words occupy my thoughts and I cannot escape them. On occasion, when that happens, my reflections circling around these powerful intrusions sometimes provide inspired insights. Here is one example, when words about love from a science fiction novel reminded me of words of love from an early Christian theologian.

The quote from the work of science fiction was "Love as thou wilt." I knew this was similar to a quote from Augustine of Hippo so I had to take the time to research and find the exact wording, which is as follows, "Once for all, then, a short precept is given thee: Love, and do what thou wilt: whether thou hold thy peace, through love hold thy peace; whether thou cry out, through love cry out; whether thou correct, through love correct; whether thou spare, through love do thou spare: let the root of love be within, of this root can nothing spring but what is good."

The great qualifier in this statement is the comma that comes after the word love. Without the comma people are simply given, with vagaries of interpretation, permission to love and do whatever they please. But the comma changes things! It makes it so that we are given the calling, the commission, perhaps even the command, to love. Then, within the context of that love we take action, whatever it may be. However, whatever action we take, it is action rooted in love. And being rooted in that love, it is good. It is the reality then, that loves motivates and moves us.

Love, and do what thou wilt.

6 - LORD'S PRAYER

Classical Seven Ring Labyrinth in Winter

Sometimes when I walk the classical seven ring labyrinth I use the seven petitions of the Lord's Prayer to help me focus my thoughts. During each circuit of the labyrinth I focus my thoughts on one of the petitions as I wind my way in. This prayer is an all encompassing prayer which touches all aspects of living and volumes have been written in exposition of it.

I may not have anything unique to add to that mass of material, but what struck me as I walked this morning was that while my walk through the labyrinth is fundamentally a solitary venture in physical activity which engages me in the world around me, the

Lord's Prayer is fundamentally a communal prayer which engages me with God, this creation, and humanity. While I may be walking alone, and praying alone, living is about "us".

Even if, for some reason, you should happen to be alone today, remember you are not "alone," for all who are praying this prayer are with you.

7 - LOVE IS A DECISION

Marriage of Friends

I walked into the night and was greeted by the stars above and the bright, nearly full, moon reflecting off a new-fallen dusting of snow into millions of crystalline points of light. What a beautiful and soul-filling delight. But now I had decisions to make. Which path would I take? Which labyrinth would I walk?

The thought of decisions filled my mind, and I was reminded of a lesson I learned many years ago, but one I re-learn every day. Love is a decision.

Say what one might about emotion, passion, and desire (I'll not deny those play a role in love) but the essence of what love revolves around - is decision.

Before I walk into the labyrinth, I have to decide to do it. No one is forcing me. I may be invited into it, but I cannot be forced. So also with love. I am not forced, but I may be invited. However, I still have to make the decision to step forward and to love. Once I enter the labyrinth the path is laid out before me and the promise of my progress is sure, but there comes the point when I complete the walk by exiting the labyrinth. At that time, I will have to make the decision to re-enter. So also with love. Each day I must make the decision to enter the path, to love, and each day I am rewarded by the journey.

Will you make the decision this day, to love?

8 - SEVEN GENERATIONS

Classical Seven Ring Labyrinth in Autumn

The seven ring classical labyrinth has a structure that invites several forms of prayer. I previously mentioned praying the seven petitions of the Lord's Prayer as one walks their way in or out. Another beneficial reflective practice is use the Native American tradition of remembering the seven generations. This tradition calls on us to respect, honor, and learn from the seven generations that have preceded us and to protect, care for, and live in ways that will be beneficial for the seven generations that follow us.

Sometimes I will enter the labyrinth, prayerfully finding my way into communion with God, and then on the way out I will place myself at the center of seven generations.

The first ring on the way out is a prayer for myself and for my generation - that we might live wisely and in fellowship with God, the creation, and each other.

Each ring reverses direction, so as I move into the second ring I break with thoughts of my generation, and I consider my parent's generation. I give thanks for the world they left us and the sacrifices and gifts they gave us.

The direction shifts, and the third ring brings thoughts and prayers for my children and their generation. We have given them life and direction. I pray that the course we have set them upon is good, and right, and just.

Again the direction shifts, and the fourth ring calls for thoughts of our grandparents and their generation. They were those people in my life with age and wisdom honed with experience of lives lived full of hardships and happiness.

The direction turns, and the fifth ring fills with thoughts of grandchildren. What joy and pleasure they bring, and how deeply I pray that my generation might be a witness to them of lives filled with faith, hope, and love.

And again the direction shifts, and in the sixth ring I move back further in time to a generation I never knew personally, but to a generation to which I give thanks, for they took risks and forged a future for their families in a new land.

Another turn brings the seventh ring and the final steps outward, and I consider the generation to come - my grandchildren's children. What kind of world are we leaving for them and the unknown generations to come?

9 - RECOGNIZING ROOTS

Baltic Labyrinth

One labyrinth I walk is a traditional Baltic Labyrinth, so-called because some examples of these from times long ago have been found in the Baltic region.

It is a different type of labyrinth because you come out of it a different way from the way you enter it - yet still at the same place.

I use this labyrinth to consider my roots. As I walk the path I reflect upon where I have come from. I consider the different roots and experiences that have made me who I am. This includes my mother and father - and the traditions and families they came from, my religious and spiritual traditions - they certainly affect how I think and how I view life, the communities I have been a part of - what an impact they have had on me, and even national and world events - which have shaped the times of my life.

When I use this method, the journey into this labyrinth essentially becomes a deep reflection on the past. It is a necessary journey. You can not know your way to where you are going, if you do not know where you have come from and where you are.

After being grounded in my roots, and seeing more clearly where I am, I spend some time in the inner sanctuary of this spiral and consider what future directions I wish to take in my daily living and even for the span of my life. Then I start my walk out. This part of the Baltic Labyrinth is a much shorter path, and almost immediately I am thrust out of it and into the world - my roots have given me understanding and direction. I go forward with purpose.

10 - NOTHING TO SEE

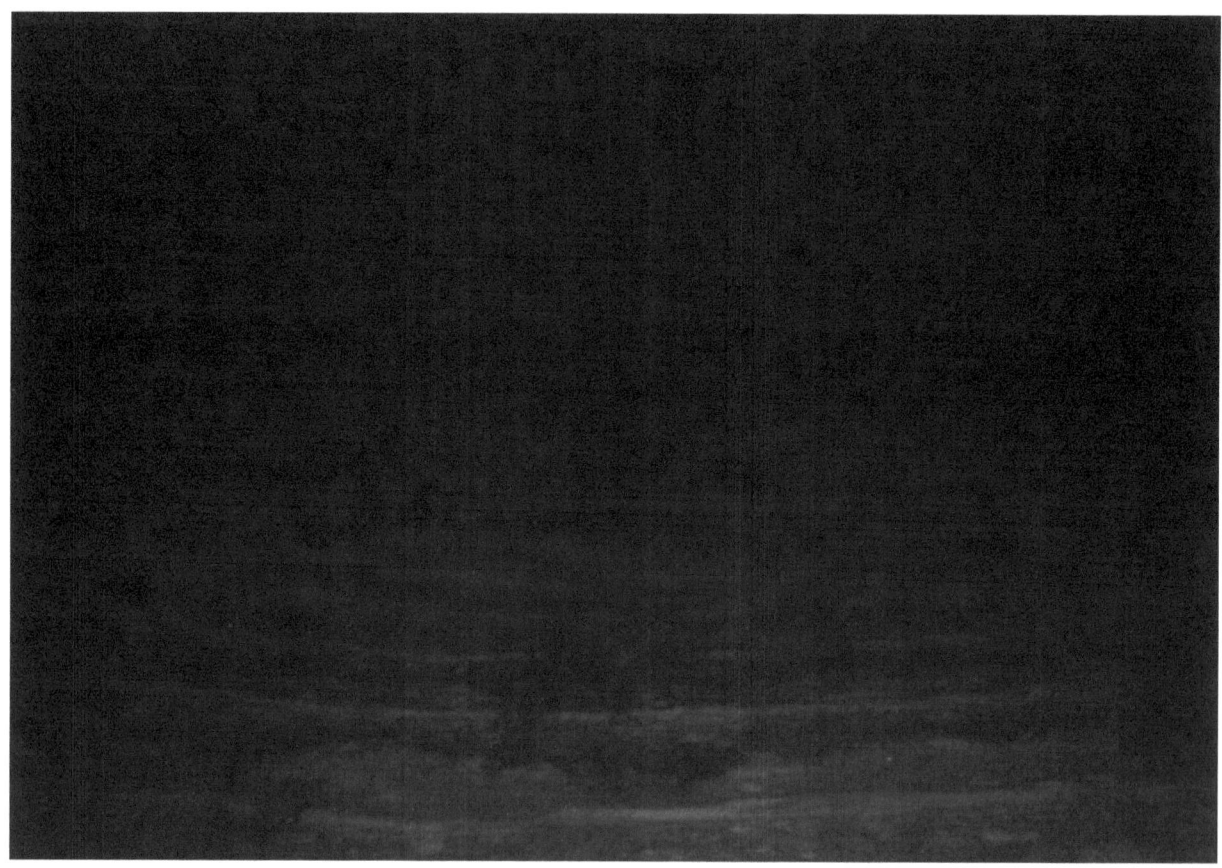

Now I See But Dimly

There was nothing to see as I walked in meditation this morning. The stars and moon were blanketed by the thick clouds. There was no sun yet to brighten the sky. The dark lay heavy on the earth. And so I walked. Nothing.
Some days are like that.

Nothing to see. No great visions. No teasing insights.

Nothing.

But that was alright. Because life was all right. I was alive. I was walking. I was walking with the divine presence. What need was there for anything else? And so I walked.

Nothing, but everything.

Some days are like that.

11 - SILENT NIGHT

Morning Star

I walked in the hours before dawn of December 24, and my soul was warmed.

I thought of Christmas stories and traditions as I walked in the stillness of the night.

Yes, Virginia, there is a Silent Night. Through the scintillating starlight I walked this holy night. The temperatures dipped below zero and the wind stood still. I kept moving in order to keep myself warm. But while I walked, there were those moments when the beauty of the heavenly host of stars compelled me to stop and be still, and listen for the voice of God.

From some of the recesses of my memory I heard the words of Psalm 46, "Be still and know that I am God." Yes, we tend to be so busy with all our movements through our days and lives, that we sometimes start to wonder if there is anything holy, or divine, or greater than ourselves. We try to warm ourselves with ourselves.

Be still, and behold that which is greater than thyself.

In the stillness of this silent night our souls are warmed.

12 - AND HEAVEN AND NATURE SING

Singing Pines

In the starlight I walked, ere the moon took flight giving glory to this night; and as I walked I heard three distinct, yet harmonious songs.

There was a stiff breeze which pushed the windchill below zero, but I was warm from the physical activity and from the song that heaven and nature sang. I must confess, that even though I was walking for the exercise, I stopped on occasion because I couldn't resist the moments of just listening to the music around me.

One song grew strongest when I paused near a grove of Red Pine trees. I am no musician and I hesitate to try to describe the strong brushing song of those needles and branches in the wind, but it energized me.

Then I came to a copse of White Pine trees. There the trees sang with a softer swooshing sound which soothed and satisfied me.

Next, I walked through those tall prairie grasses, and heard them whisper urgently of moving on as the snow which lay upon the ground tumbled from drift to drift.

Three songs, distinct, yet one - a trinity of harmony. My soul is soothed, and I may sleep and dream in peace.

Is there a message here? Perhaps, if we would let there be. Can we hear the world around us sing? Do we hear the voice of God when heaven and nature sing? Do we let it soothe our souls?

13 - SEEING THE CENTER

Classical Labyrinth at Sunset

One thing I have noticed about walking the classical labyrinth is that you have your vision focused on the center of the labyrinth only when you enter the labyrinth, and then again when you actually get to the center. While you are making the circuits the center hangs in your peripheral vision, and when you make the turns the center just quickly flashes through your field of vision.

So often, that is the way my daily journey progresses. I have a vision and understanding of who I am and what I want to become as I begin the day. But then the activities of my day begin and my sight is pulled to many other places. I know who I want to be and where I want to go, but I can only see that on the edges and in flashes.

Until.

Until I finally reach the end of the day when I can lay in silent reflection of the day, and see again the center, and be that which I have come to be.

14 - BEST TIME OF THE DAY

Autumn Dawn from the Labyrinth

I have a couple of friends who share my thought that the best time of the day is that time quite early in the morning (or in the minds of some - that time very late at night.) This is the time we rejoice in this creation by doing our meditations as we exercise our bodies, though miles apart. Sometimes later in the day, we occasionally take pleasure in sharing with each other the experiences of those moments.

These are the hours when most of those around us are sleeping, and it appears that the world itself is sleeping.

But those of us who walk and pray in those hours know the truth. The world is not asleep, but quiet, and waiting. It is as though time has paused to allow the eyes of God to survey all that has been in the hours that have passed, to witness all that is in the moment of the now, and to gaze into all that might come to be in the approaching day.

A watchful waiting hangs in the air. Soon the breaking dawn will start to touch the horizon. Soon the voice of field and forest, and of town and city, will come humming to life. But for now, for this moment, there lies on the land a stillness of anticipation.

Can you feel the eyes of God waiting with us? On us?

What will this new day bring? What challenges, hardships, relationships, and pleasures lie before us? I can hardly wait!

But I wait. For a few moments of time - I wait, and I anticipate. What a gift this is - to wait.

15 - THE JOURNEY IN AND THE JOURNEY OUT

Late Summer Dawn on Vermillion Lake

The labyrinth has helped me to understand the principle (and to apply it to my living) that both the journey into the divine presence and also the journey back out into the world are important.

I come to the labyrinth full of myself, my problems, my thoughts. I come so self-centered that the world, the sun, the stars - the entire universe - seems to revolve around me.

Bishop Tutu of South Africa once posed the reflective question, "How can you expect for God to fill you with the Spirit, when you are so full of yourself?"

As I begin the walk into the labyrinth, seeking insight - seeking the divine, I look at myself; and I find myself failed, and flawed, and frail. I am not at all the center of the universe. My layers peel away as I am drawn into the center.

Sometimes this exercise in reflection and humility is painful - and sometimes it is releasing and joyful. I let go of myself. I empty myself. I am open to be filled by the Spirit.

Ah, but the journey out! Now, the Divine has room to work in my existence and as I travel outward I can be filled with love of God, love for this creation, love for my fellow children of God. Being so filled, I am able to go out and live in the fullness of my humanity and share this love.

The labyrinth has stripped me of "me" and fills me to be who I was created to be.

16 - CLOUDY MORNING SUNRISE

Geese Migrating on Cloudy Morning

Walking the labyrinth during a cloudy morning sunrise reaffirmed the knowledge that you cannot see the sun rise when skies are filled with clouds. Yet the sun does rise, and yet one does know that the sun has risen for light has come.

I walked in the minutes before the sun was predicted to rise and it was dark. I could but dimly see my path. Then slowly the light began to brighten and the world around me was revealed. Moment by moment greater definition and detail of this creation was placed on display. I could not see the sun, yet I knew the sun had risen.

Walking the labyrinth during the sunrise of a cloudy day can be a metaphor for life. We may feel as though we live and walk in darkness. But there is light, and that light enters our darkness and overcomes it. Some people may call this "enlightenment", others may call it by other words depending upon their faith tradition. My tradition calls it "Christ." The Light of the World enters our humanity bringing light to the darkness which surrounds us. We can see life in fullness (the good and the not so good) and we can see the paths which lie before us - the potentials and the problems.

We may not always see the sun, the clouds may hide it from view, but we know that it is there. We feel the power of its light and we can live in the light.

17 - EPIPHANIES

Revelation at Dawn

I arise early – before the slightest hint of dawn touches the eastern horizon;

And I walk – following the paths and labyrinths which surround me;

And I open my soul - hoping for renewal and insight for the day;

And I listen – for the sounds of creation and for the voice of God;

And I look – for even by light of moon or star there is sight given;

And I confess – the faults and failures which lie within me;

And I pray - for wisdom which lies beyond my simple self;

And I dream – of that which might yet be;

And I am given – grace to still my soul;

And I am given – peace to calm my heart;

And I am given – thoughts to stir my mind;

And I am given – purpose for my living;

And so – I arise today.

18 - WALKING OR SILENCE

Moonrise

This day I thought that I walked in silence.

The world around me was silent, but alas, I was not. My sound, that reverberated through the frigid air, was the sound of my snowshoes crunching on the crusty, snow-packed path of the labyrinth. However, when I stopped - then there was silence. I wanted to enjoy the peace and utter silence of this place, but if I did - if I was still and made no sound or movement - then I made no progress.

Then I started to wonder about my need of making progress and achieving a goal. This prompted me to ponder about which was more important: to let the stillness of a moment of peace wash over me, or to be striving toward and attaining a worthy goal? And would my answer to that question be the same if answered tomorrow, or the next day?

Which would you have in your life? Inner peace, or progress on your life's journey.

Are they mutually exclusive?

It is something to think about.

19 - STARLIGHT

Sky Filled with Stars

As I began my early morning walk along the paths this morning I was greeted with the view of the stars stretching across the sky from horizon to horizon. I took the time to look up in wonder and appreciation. Even though I walked with care, using my walking staff for support, I was graced and enlightened by the starlight.

But then the clouds rolled in, until there was only an occasional glimpse of a star that filtered through. And I thought - how much this is like my daily walk through life. I start the day with clarity, and sometimes even insight, but then as the day goes on those become covered - clouded over - by the multitude of mundane trivialities before me. And I lose sight of the vision.

But there is a remedy. I have in my memory the vision of the stars touching the rim of the world. I can pause, call forth that vision, and return to the clarity and purpose of my living. So I would do today.

20 - LETTING THE PATH PULL YOU FORWARD

Ski Track Near the Labyrinths

This morning's pre-dawn exercise began with several cross-country skiing circuits of the paths which surround the labyrinths, and provided me with a reminder of trust. There was plenty of light, for the clouds had not yet diminished the light of the moon and the sun was just beginning to lighten the eastern horizon. I could make out the parallel tracks of the ski trail running before me, so I pushed off and began my meditation. What satisfaction there is to be smoothly gliding across a moonlit snowy landscape!

But I noticed that when I focused on looking at the tracks and making sure my stride would keep me in them I would lose sight of the beauty surrounding me. I focused so narrowly on the track that I surrendered the gift of seeing the wonders around me. However, when I let go and let the path pull me forward and trusted the firmly cut grooves of the tracks embedded in the snow, I had no need to look down and watch the path. I could look around me and revel in the moment.

Are you following a sure path in life? When you are, you can look up, look around, and revel in the moment. Let the path of love and truth pull you forward. Trust the path and enjoying the living.

21 - SACRED

A Sacred Sunrise

As I was walking what I sometimes call the sacred spiral, I started thinking about what is sacred, and what makes something sacred.

It was my intention, as I walked, to reflect on the question, what makes something "sacred"? That soon shifted to include what is "sacred"? I did a lot of thinking, but I didn't really come up with how to put my thoughts into words at that time.

After several days of reflection and discussion with friends, I came up with the following comment.

Regarding the seeking of "sacred." I may not have a definition (as the saying goes, "I may not be able to define it, but I know it when I see it"), but I do have some recent personal experiences of the sacred:

- the spontaneous laughter of delight erupting when walking in the cold night air and seeing the moon and stars in all their glory
- a woman making sure a freezing family gets heat back in their house
- a mother cradling her child
- the smile of a friend in the morning
- the "love ya" of a loved one
- the stillness of a labyrinth
- the unsolicited hug from a grandchild
- tears shed over others' pain
- a glorious color-infused sunrise

After several more days of reflection, as I walked the three ring labyrinth, I visualized an answer to this as a trinity. Thoughts of the sacred melded into a three-fold revelation.

The sacred involves place. It is connected to creation - that which the Creator has brought into being and which is filled with goodness and the wonder all of that is (tangible and intangible).

Second, the sacred revolves around relationships. It is expressed and lived out in relationships with the divine and with others.

Third, the sacred evolves time. We normally understand time chronologically, but there are moments which differ from this understanding of time. My tradition calls this "kairos" time. It is when special moments, or events, transcend and suspend normal time.

So, what is sacred? The spirit blows where, with whom, and when it wills.

22 - WALKING STAFF

One of My Walking Staffs

When I go out walking the paths and labyrinths I usually take a walking staff with me. It came in very useful this morning as I walked, because the melting temperatures of the previous days and then the current cold snap left the paths icy and slippery. The steady support of the staff enabled me to walk securely and safely.

The paths of the labyrinth are unchanging. The goal when the path is followed is sure. But the conditions of the path vary with time and weather. It is a metaphor for life.

The staff is a part of that metaphor. It is something outside of myself that gives support, strength, and security.

For some people their "staff" in life is the sacred writings of their spiritual tradition, for others it might be solid friends and confidants, for others is might be a supportive family, for others it might be the witness of their faith community. There are several possibilities for that which might be a person's staff in their spiritual journey.

What might be your "staff?"

23 - TUNNEL VISION

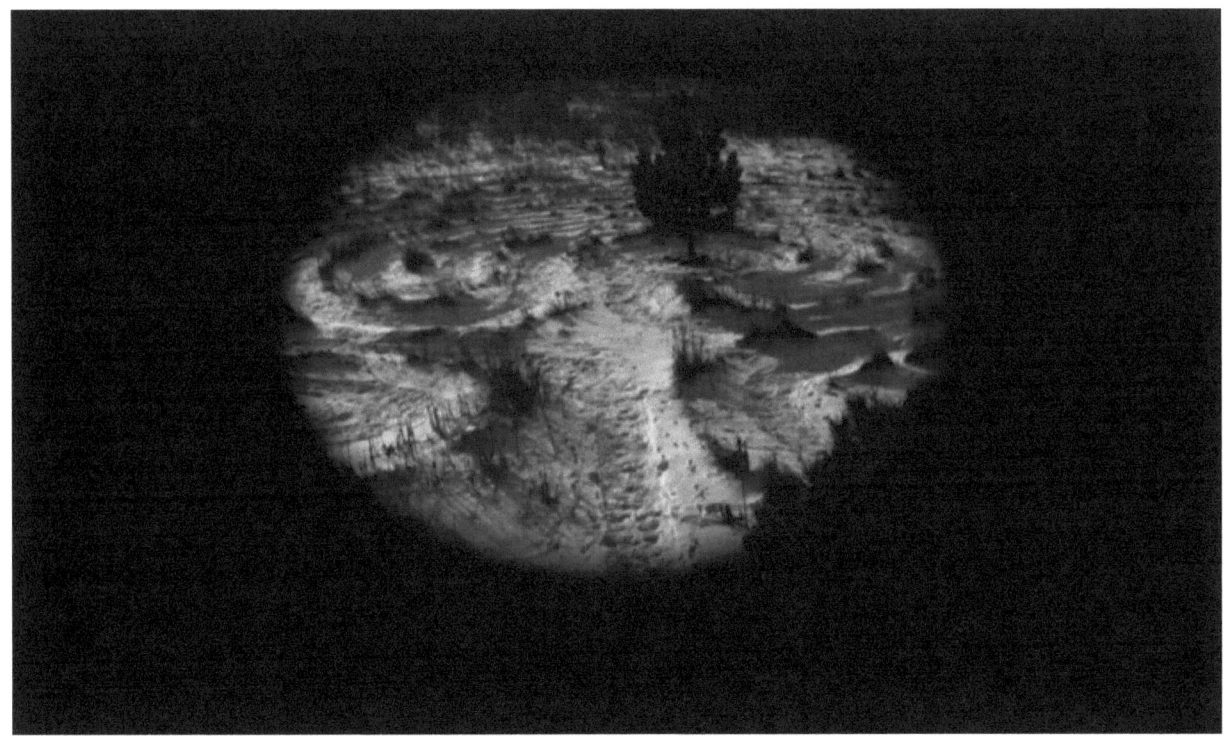

Tunnel Vision on a Cold Day

I walked with tunnel vision this morning. Some members of my family were wondering if I was slightly "touched" because when I went out to walk this morning the temperature was -12 degrees, with a windchill of -27 degrees.

I will admit that I am slightly different, however, I do know how to dress for the weather, and I did cut my walk a few minutes short. I was actually quite comfortable. But I walked with tunnel vision. I was so bundled up that I only had a small hole to see and breath through. For me, this morning, tunnel vision was good.

Some days, having tunnel vision in our spiritual lives can also be good. The hardships and difficulties surrounding us may be so harsh at a given time that we survive by going deep within ourselves. However, when we do, we find that God is there.

25 - ENDINGS

Ending of an Autumn Day from a Labyrinth

As I walked the labyrinths this delightfully cold and starlit morning, I wondered about endings. Today is a day some have predicted to be the end of the world because of an ancient Mayan calendar, so I wondered as I wandered into the labyrinth - where is the end?

The end was not the beginning. So much lay before me.

The end was not the innermost core. For there must be the journey out.

The end was not the exit from the labyrinth. For every exit is only the invitation to re-enter and to continue on.

The question of today may be the question of every day: Is today the end?

It is but one step in a continuing journey. Enjoy this day of your journey. It may be a new day, it may be the end of a previous day, but it is not the end of all. Live this day to its fullest.

26 - NOT DEAD

Empty Milkweed Pods in the Center of the Labyrinth

Last summer, in the very center of one of the labyrinths I groom, a milkweed plant started to grow. I could have easily mowed it down, but it sort of struck my fancy, so I let it grow and I trimmed the grasses around it. It became a focal point for that labyrinth.

When autumn came, it opened its pods and the silky seeds were blown away in the wind and scattered afar. Now those seed pods stand empty to the snow and biting winds of winter. There, in the center of this labyrinth, thrusting itself out of the deepening snow, is this dead milkweed plant.

However, this is no symbol of death, and winter is not the season of death.

The empty seed pods are a symbol of life. Those seeds have been planted, near and far. They are only awaiting the heat and moisture which will burst them sprouting forth. Winter is a season pregnant with anticipation for the wild and exuberant growth of spring.

So as I walk, and see the barren landscape, and feel the sharp, cold bite of winter winds, I center my thoughts on the center of this labyrinth, and I see the promise of new life.

I am reminded to see through that which might seem barren and bitter, and see the love and promise of life around me. What seeds, just lying there, waiting, will germinate in the near future.

I can hardly wait to see.

27 - EYE ON THE PATH

Twists and Turns of a Labyrinth

I needed to keep an eye on the path as I walked today. It was so enjoyable to be gazing up and around because as I walked the clouds raced to the horizons leaving the sky glimmering with thousands of points of starlight. It felt like a glimpse of the divine was being offered to me. However, a labyrinth is filled with twists and turns. The path is not hidden, but if you are not aware of the turns then you can walk right off the path. So when I had my eyes lifted up, I lost my way on the path. I needed to keep a eye on the labyrinth path as I walked.

My life is like that sometimes. I have good intentions. I can even get carried away by that which is wonderful and good. But when I do that, I can run the risk of stumbling off the path of goodness that is leading me through life. I need to keep an eye on the path.

So what a delightful paradox. Some days I need to be reminded to lift my eyes and see the wonder which lies around me. Other days I need to be reminded to keep my eyes on the path lest I wander off. And yet other days I need to be reminded of both.

28 - PASS IT ON

What Joy in Giving Something Away

My last couple of days of meditation have been focused on thoughts of living a life of love, and of giving and receiving. I think my thoughts can best be shared by telling a couple of stories linked together.

A couple of Sundays ago we went to a local diner after worship. As we sat at the table waiting for our food to come, my wife leaned in close, motioned toward a table of six elderly women on the other side of the diner (none of whom we knew), and whispered to me, "We're going to pay for their meal." It made me smile because I knew what she was doing. She was "passing it on."

Now we shift back in time to when the two of us were recently married. I was in graduate school and we had NO money. We literally had so little money in our pockets we didn't know where our next meal would come from. Then, a envelope came sliding under our door with some cash in it.

We figured that some of our friends, who knew of our situation, must have given us this gift. However, I was pretty proud and didn't want to accept charity. So we went to our friends to return the gift. They would not accept it back, or even acknowledge that they gave it to us. But they did give us a lesson in giving (and receiving). They suggested we graciously accept it and use it, because obviously whoever gave it to us wanted us to have it with no strings attached, but that at some point in the future we might "pass it on" to someone we thought could use it and, if the opportunity arose, to invite them to "pass it on" in their future.

During the course of our lives, we have passed that initial gift on numerous times. Sometimes it has been anonymous, sometimes the recipients know who we are. It is amazing how that initial gift has multiplied, and it is amazing how each time we (the givers) feel as though we have been blessed more than the recipients.

Now, back to the six elderly ladies. We told our waitress that we would be taking care of the ladies' bill, but that they were not to know who had paid it for them. Then we sat back and enjoyed our meal. What a delight it was to see the ladies expressions when they were told someone had paid for their meal. I'm sure that to this day they are still trying to figure it out, and while I was not able to invite them to "pass it on", I can't help but think that our generosity may bless them and inspire them. In my mind, this is living a life of love.

I wonder who will be the next to receive a such a gift? And I wonder who will be the next to give such a gift when their time comes?

29 - PASS IT ON

Some of the Symbols and Tokens I Use

Lots of symbols came to mind this morning. I am a person who uses symbolic items to help me remember things and to help me refocus my thoughts throughout the day.

Even though I normally walk the labyrinth sometime during the day, I will also usually be wearing a labyrinth ring, or pendant as a tangible reminder which helps me to refocus my thoughts and re-energizes me in the path I have chosen for the day.

The items I use do not have power in and of themselves, other than what I have given them in the ability to affect me and bring me to a renewed sense of awareness.

I have sometimes taken pride in my memory and my ability to recall information, but I find that all too frequently I forget the truly important spiritual things as I am engaged in my daily living. I need to be reminded - frequently - or I lose the spiritual dimension of the moment. When I lose the spiritual dimension, then the rest of my living goes askew. To be whole, I need almost continuing re- focusing and renewal.

So I use small items that I can wear or carry in my pockets. They have the meaning, and power of renewal, that I give them.

Can you find some symbols that would help you be reminded and renewed in your spiritual journey?

30 - DOING GOOD

Dawn of a New Day

Is doing good doing God?

I have come to believe that when we do good we are the hands and heart of the divine embracing this world.

Many religious traditions have some sort of creation story which in some manner expresses the thought that, "God saw what God had made, and it was good." God and goodness go together.

How will you greet this new day? Will you see it as a good and gracious gift of God? As something to be treasured, nurtured, and cherished? Will you see your opportunities during this day to be moments to extend this good gift to the world and people around you? Will the goodness of the divine fill your heart and extend your hands in sharing that goodness with others?

Will you do good today?

ACKNOWLEDGEMENTS

All text and photographs by Joel Kreger

Author may be contacted at: kregerjoel@gmail.com

ISBN 978-0-9889514-9-5
© 2013 Joel Kreger

www.ingramcontent.com/pod-product-compliance
Lightning Source LLC
Chambersburg PA
CBHW042007100426
42738CB00039B/40